Keep Kids Safe

A Parent's Guide to Child Safety

Quality Life Resources

KEEP KIDS SAFE
A Parent's Guide to Child Safety

2000 Copyright Aid Association for Lutherans

All rights reserved. Except for brief quotations in critical articles or reviews, no part of this book may be reproduced in any manner without prior written permission from the publisher. Write to: Permissions, AAL QualityLife Resources, 4321 N. Ballard Road, Appleton, WI 54919-0001.

Library of Congress Cataloging-in-Publication Data Card Number: 00-104655

KEEP KIDS SAFE
First Edition

Includes bibliographical references

1. Safety, Children 2. Accidents, Children 3. Safety, Home

I. Title.
ISBN 0-9701509-1-1 (Paper: alk. paper)

Manufactured in the U.S.A.

03 02 01 00 1 2 3 4 5 6 7 8 9 10

TABLE OF CONTENTS

SECTION I - Home Safe Home 2
Fall-related injury prevention 2
Reducing the Risk of Sudden Infant Death Syndrome (SIDS) 6
Preventing fire and burns 6
Poison prevention 12
Preventing choking 16
Miscellaneous hazards 18

SECTION II - Safe and Sound Outside the Home 22
Motor vehicle accident prevention 22
Child abduction prevention 27
Vacation safety 30

SECTION III - At Home or Away 34
Preventing drowning 34
Internet safety 36
Guns and safety 37
Sporting and recreation safety 39

SECTION IV - If All Else Fails 44
Calling 911 44
First aid and CPR 44
Conclusion 45

SUMMARY 46
Family safety checklist 46
Bibliography 47
Resources for additional information 48
Index 50

INTRODUCTION

Accidental injury, more than disease, is the leading cause of death among children. Accidents can happen to children suddenly and without warning. Some seem unavoidable. But families who take common-sense precautions are likely to prevent them or at least to minimize their seriousness.

Injuries to children up to age 4 usually occur in settings controlled by their parents. By learning ways to keep our homes safe, we become better equipped to prevent injury to our young children.

Children ages 5 to 12 need to learn safety when they are on their own much of the time. This means we need to teach them skills that will protect them as pedestrians, bike riders, and automobile passengers. We also need to provide them with safe play areas and protective sports equipment.

This book's purpose is to help you keep your children safe. Of course, despite the best advice about safety, there are no guarantees—no matter how diligent, careful, and loving we are, accidents do happen. The book offers you a collection of practical, hands-on advice to remind you of some of the most common and easily countered threats to children.

As a parent, you are your child's best teacher. So think ahead and look for opportunities to teach your child and set a good example whenever the chance arises. For example, a simple walk to the store might be a good time to help your child learn the rules of pedestrian safety. A family camping trip is an opportunity to discuss fire hazards and water safety.

The book is divided into three main sections:

I. Preventing accidents that occur at home.

II. Preventing accidents that occur away from home.

III. Preventing accidents that could occur in either.

After these three accident prevention sections, a fourth section addresses emergency procedures if an accident occurs. The book concludes with a summary Family Safety Checklist that reviews prevention tools.

SECTION I

Home Safe Home

When most of us think of home, we have comforting thoughts of warmth, familiarity and security. It can be hard to move from these emotional markers and examine our homes carefully for the everyday dangers they present to our kids. But research shows that most young children who have been injured or killed by a fall, fire, poisoning, or choking were in their homes at the time. Let's look at how we can help prevent accidents in the home.

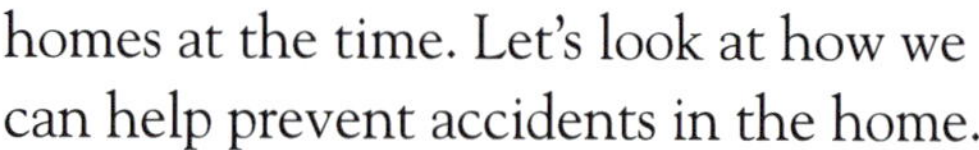

Fall-related Injury Prevention

Kids love to climb on things. Maybe it's the result of an innate need to move toward higher ground. Most likely it's because it's just plain fun.

But it's fun that can be hazardous. According to the National Safe Kids Campaign, falls are the most common reason for a child's hospital stay or emergency room visit. Falls often result in head injuries or broken limbs upon landing.

Honey, when did the baby learn to roll over?

Typically, babies learn to roll over sometime between 3 and 5 months. One of the most common baby falls occurs when the parent who didn't think her daughter could roll over, turns away from her for a second and discovers yes, indeed, she can. Another common scenario for a fall is when Dad places junior in the middle of the queen-size bed. Looking through his closet for an ironed shirt and hearing a thump and a wail, he realizes junior needs a king-size.

Never leave your baby unattended, even for a second, when she is on an above-ground surface. Strap your infant into the stroller, high chair, or infant seat. Remove the bumpers and large stuffed animals from the crib as soon as your baby can pull herself up. She could use these as boosts to climb up and over. Also at this time, lower the mattress to its lowest position and double-check that the drop side is locked in the highest position. And because kids can overcome even the most stringent precautions, place a thick rug underneath the crib to soften a fall you can't prevent.

But when the crib mattress is at its lowest position and the top rail is below your child's nipples, or when your child is 35 inches in height, it's time for him to move into a bed. Place the bed against a wall and use a guardrail on the other side. The top of the upper guardrail should be at least 5 inches above the upper mattress.

Climb every mountain ... and bookcase ... and couch ...

As parents, we treasure our child's first step ... and then look back longingly on those days when we didn't have to view our household furnishings as things our daughter was about to pull down on herself or jump off of.

As babies become mobile, crawling, pulling themselves up on furniture, and finally walking, the living areas of our homes often go from *Better Homes and Gardens*-quality to *Better Bare Essentials*. This is the time to store glass objects, pottery, and anything breakable. Besides the frustration of losing a valued object, the risk of a child cutting herself on a jagged edge of a broken vase is too great.

Get down on your hands and knees and check for hazards from your baby's point of view. Check that nothing can topple over on her. ***Heavy bookcases, stereo shelves, and grandfather clocks are often unstable—they should be secured to the wall before your infant starts to crawl.*** It also helps to cover sharp furniture edges with cushioned, adhesive corner covers. Always push chairs in under the dining room and kitchen table. Close dresser or chest drawers all the way to keep toddlers from falling in or tripping on them. Remind your kids and their friends that beds are not trampolines—don't allow them to jump on the beds.

Bring all the sun in, but keep windows closed

Babies have heavy heads relative to their body weight and if they lean out a window, they are likely to topple over and fall out. The National Safe Kids Campaign says that ***a window open as little as 4 inches presents a hazard for a child under 10.*** Child-accessible windows should be covered with child safety screens (an ordinary window screen only keeps bugs out; a child safety screen is sturdier and keeps kids in) or fitted with window locks that are childproof. Keep furniture away from windows—denying access can be your best defense. You can guard against head bumps and cuts from low-hanging picture windows and sliding glass doors by placing stickers on them to alert your child that they are glass.

Never leave your child alone on a deck, fire escape, or balcony. And when you are with her on an outside raised surface, check that the slats on the fencing are sturdy and close enough together to prevent her from squeezing through.

Down the up staircase

Parents who live in two-story homes and who have infants have no need to enroll in a step aerobics class. They live a personal training program—climbing up stairs and down all day long, often toting a 15-pound baby, a laundry basket, or a bag of groceries, rarely empty-handed.

But things get even more complicated when baby starts to crawl or inch her way along the floor on her belly. At this point, if you have a flight of stairs in your home, gates are necessary to keep your crawling or beginning-to-walk child from tumbling down, though they are never a substitute for your attention.

Attach the gate to a wall at the top of the stairs—a pressure gate at the top isn't strong enough. Also, avoid accordion-style gates with large openings—it's too easy for a toddler to trap his neck in the holes. The American Academy of Pediatrics (AAP) recommends a gate with slats no more than $2\frac{3}{8}$ inches apart. Pressure gates made of plastic mesh or netting may be used at the bottom of the stairs, but place the pressure bar on the side away from your child, so he can't step up on it or pry it open.

Remind older children and guests to keep the gates closed at all times. Keep stairs well-lit and free of clutter to protect everyone in the house. Move furniture with hard, sharp edges out of traffic patterns. The

coffee table is often the culprit in an injury to a young child who is learning to walk. You can also buy cushioned corner and edge protectors for furniture. Guard against accidents by teaching your children to wear shoes and socks or go barefoot—socks alone turn uncarpeted stairs into a slippery hazard. And you'll lessen the chance of slips altogether if the house rules state clearly: ***No game-playing on the stairs.***

Beware of baby walkers also—doctors are warning that they can do more harm than good. The problem is that kids careen down the stairs in them. In 1997, more than 16,000 children were taken to the emergency room for baby-walker-related accidents. The American Academy of Pediatrics does not recommend using baby walkers. Even when children don't fall down the stairs in them, some walkers tip over easily, causing bruises, bumps, and sometimes even fractures. And don't think that just because you're watching, your baby will be safe in a walker. According to the National Safe Kids Campaign, 80 percent of injuries to young children in baby walkers happen *while* they are being supervised. Babies learn to walk best the old-fashioned way—by graduating from sitting up, to crawling, to pulling themselves up to a stand, and then tumbling down on their bottoms to start all over again.

TAKING ACTION to prevent falls:

- Never leave your baby unattended, even for a second, when she is on an above-ground surface.
- Bookcases and stereo or TV shelves are often unstable—they should be secured to the wall before your baby starts to crawl.
- Windows should be covered with child safety screens or fitted with child-proof window locks, but safe for fire egress.
- Fit stairways with secure gates, and enforce the house rule: No game-playing on the stairs.

Reducing the Risk of Sudden Infant Death Syndrome (SIDS)

The AAP says that one or two newborns out of every 1000 die in their sleep. These infants are generally between the fourth and 16th weeks of life, are generally well-cared-for and have no signs of illness.

Their autopsies also show no signs of illness, so the term Sudden Infant Death Syndrome (SIDS) is used to describe their deaths.

Since 1992, the AAP has recommended that healthy infants be placed on their backs when being put down to sleep.

You can find out about additional ways to reduce your infant's risk of SIDS by calling the toll-free "Back to Sleep" campaign line at (800) 505-CRIB. You should also discuss this with your baby's doctor, since individual factors may affect the preventive measures which can be taken.

Preventing Fire and Burns

The National Safe Kids Campaign reports that fires and burns are the third leading cause of accidental injury-related deaths among children, killing nearly 800 children and injuring nearly 47,000 children ages 14 and under every year. But the chances of a child dying or being injured in a residential fire can be cut in half by properly installing and using smoke detectors. Parents need to use common sense and safe practices in the kitchen and other areas of the house to prevent burns and fire, and equally important, families need to practice fire drills that show children how to escape safely from the house should a fire begin.

Beware when someone's in the kitchen

Young children ages 6 months to 2 years are beginning to master mobility, but they don't have a clue as to what's safe and what's not. When they are in the kitchen, they need constant supervision. They will reach out (if you're holding them) or up (if they're underfoot) while you're cooking and upend pots of hot liquid on themselves. They will reach into open oven doors, even if you turn your back for just a second. They will grab for your coffee cup when you're holding them on your lap. ***Keep hot liquids away from children***—place pots on the back burners of the stove, with the handles facing toward the back wall, and place your coffee mug in the middle of a stable surface out of your child's reach.

As your children become more steady on their feet and begin to be able to understand household dangers, they still need supervision in the kitchen. A child 5 to 12 may be overconfident about his ability to carry hot liquids. Remind him that he needs your help with this. Don't store cookies, crackers, cereal, or any food that your child enjoys and is allowed to snack on, above the stove. A too-common scenario has a child burning himself as he reaches up to a shelf above a lit stove burner.

Many parents think it is safe to let a 6- or 7-year-old use the microwave oven on her own. But until parents decide a child is mature enough, she should never operate a microwave. Children can't be expected to remember all the rules regarding timing and safe containers all the time. The risks are varied. Kids are likely to spill hot food on themselves as they remove the container from the microwave—especially when it sits on a high counter. Steam burns are also possible when a child removes the

lid from a covered dish or opens a bag of microwaved popcorn.

Listen to Smokey, don't play with matches

Matches and cigarette lighters pose a particular danger for children. Even babies find their flame pretty and will be drawn toward playing with them. Matches should be stored in a metal container placed high out of reach. ***Children should also be taught that matches and lighters are tools, not toys, and be instructed to tell an adult if they find matches or a lighter lying around the house.*** School-age kids should be taught to handle matches safely, closing the box or matchbook before striking away from themselves and others, but they should only be allowed to light a match when an adult is present. Though the Consumer Product Safety Commission (CPSC) now requires *all* disposable lighters to be child-resistant, smokers still need to be especially careful with their lighters, and they should never leave a cigarette burning in an ashtray. When camping, be sure to watch out for stray campfire sparks. They can travel farther than you might think.

Electricity and safety—an important connection

Children like to play with electrical cords and outlets. Babies will stick things in any opening they can find, not knowing it's dangerous. Preschoolers may begin to understand the danger, but may decide to perform a "scientific" experiment by poking things into a socket in an effort to see what electricity is all about. You can help prevent electrical shock by covering unused electrical wall outlets with safety caps and never leaving a light socket without a bulb. Babies will also chew on cords.

Make sure all cords are in good condition, not loose or frayed, and don't hide extension cords under rugs where they could start a fire.

Appliances that heat up should always be out of reach of children. And don't let appliance cords dangle. Irons and curling irons can cause particularly deep burns.

As your child begins to play outside unsupervised, she must be warned against climbing trees that are near electrical wires. Teach your children that deadly electrical injuries can occur if they accidentally contact electrical power lines. Never let them fly a kite near a power line or on a rainy day. ***Teach your children that high-power sources, above ground electric transformers, and all electrical sources are dangerous.***

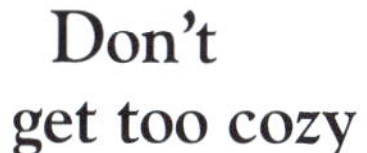

Don't get too cozy

Most of us love the idea of cozying up before a wood-burning stove or fireplace. And some of us are forced to use a space heater if our landlords are stingy with heat or our windows aren't sealed as tightly as they should be. All of these heat sources must be handled with extreme care to protect children from accidental burns and to prevent a fire from starting.

A radiant fire, whether wood, fuel, or electric, needs a safety guard. It should be of fine mesh to keep things from being poked through it and to keep sparks from flying out. It should be at least 3 feet away from the fire so it doesn't get too hot itself, and it should have a top guard to keep children from poking things behind it. You may also need a gate to block off a wood-burning stove or fireplace from a baby or toddler, but even with a gate, ***never leave a young child alone in a room where a fire is going.***

Your children learn by imitation. You must always follow safety rules and treat any fire or heat source with respect. For instance, don't let your children see you lighting a cigarette or candle from a fireplace fire. And don't keep anything too interesting above the fire source—your toddlers don't need the temptation to climb. Before winter, have a professional clean and check your home's heating system and fireplace chimney. And if you must use space heaters, keep them away from curtains, bedding, and newspapers.

Hot water can be another source of burns to your children. Dial down the water heater to 120 degrees Fahrenheit or below. At this setting, you'll have plenty of hot water for showers and dishes, but you won't risk burning your infant when he suddenly kicks on the hot water faucet as you're bathing him. The recommended bath water temperature for infants is about 100 degrees Fahrenheit.

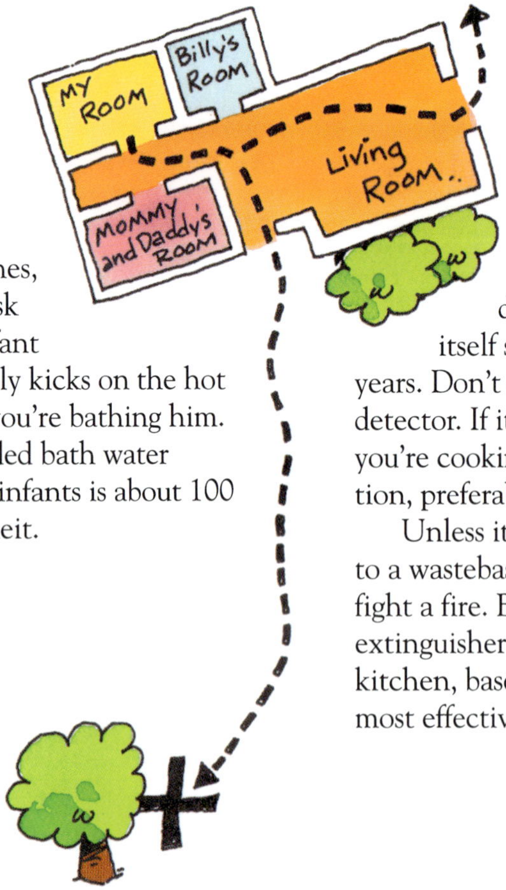

Planning your escape

No matter how careful you are, a fire may start in your home. ***It's important that you have smoke detectors, fire extinguishers, and, most important, a fire escape plan that you practice periodically with your family.***

Smoke detectors are your best defense for surviving a fire. They give you an average three extra minutes to get out of the house, and if you've planned a route ahead, that should be enough time. Install smoke detectors on every level of your home, inside each bedroom, and outside each bedroom area. Test detectors once a month and change the batteries at least once a year—choose a date you'll remember, like your birthday. The smoke detector itself should be replaced every 10 years. Don't ever disconnect your smoke detector. If it continually goes off when you're cooking, move it to a better location, preferably outside the kitchen.

Unless it is very small, like confined to a wastebasket, you shouldn't try to fight a fire. But it is wise to keep a fire extinguisher within easy reach of the kitchen, basement, and garage. The most effective all-purpose extinguishers

are rated ABC and can put out several different kinds of fires—wood, oil, or electric.

Show children 3 years and older what to do if their clothes catch on fire. Practice this drill with them:

1. **Stop. Running will make the fire burn faster. Shout, but don't run, for help.**
2. **Drop to the floor. Cover your face.**
3. **Roll back and forth to put out flames.**

Cool a burn with cool water. Never use butter on a burn.

A regularly practiced fire drill is essential for your family's safety. The practice drill should sometimes take place at night, as that is when most deadly fires occur. Each room in the house should have two escape exits, window or door. Upper levels of the house should be equipped with a portable fire ladder. Children under 6 need special attention as they may hide under a bed or in a closet when they are frightened. Teach them that this is not safe and that they should follow the escape plan instead.

Your escape plan should include these key points:

1. **Get out fast—seconds count. Phone for help from a neighbor's home, not from inside your burning house.**
2. **Stay low. Crawl under the smoke. If you can, put a moist cloth over your mouth and nose. If not, a dry cloth or your hand will still help.**
3. **Sleep with your bedroom door closed. If you wake and smell smoke, feel the door. If it's hot, don't open it, but use the second escape route from the room you're in.**
4. **Designate an outside meeting place for everyone in the family—a big tree across the street, a neighbor's front porch. This way firefighters won't be going back into the house searching for a family member who has already made it out.**
5. **Never go back inside a burning building. Not for anything.**

Children must be reminded that they can't run back for a pet or favorite toy.

TAKING ACTION to prevent fires and burns:

- Keep hot liquids away from children.
- Matches and lighters are tools, not toys—instruct your children to tell an adult if they find matches and lighters lying around the house.
- Teach your children that high-power sources, above ground electric transformers, and all electrical sources are dangerous.
- Never leave a child alone in a room where a fire is going in the fireplace or woodburning stove. Never leave a child alone near a campfire.
- Be sure your home has smoke detectors, fire extinguishers, and that your family practices a fire escape plan.

Poison Prevention

Children explore the world in a number of ways—one of them is by putting things in their mouths. According to the American Association of Poison Control Centers, in 1997 more than 1.1 million children ages 5 and under were exposed to potentially poisonous substances.

Most of us are aware of common household poisons such as medicines, drain cleaners, antifreeze and pesticides, but some of us might not be aware of less obvious dangers such as automatic dishwasher detergent, mouthwash, the houseplant in the living room window, and the disinfectant cake in the diaper pail. And all of us are susceptible to carbon monoxide poisoning and children are at risk for lead exposure through paint or water in our homes. But there are plenty of things we can do to lessen the chance of poisoning by household medicines, cleaners, plants, and environmental toxins.

A spoonful of sugar should not help the medicine go down

In the movie "Mary Poppins," super-nanny Mary uses her magical powers to make her young charges' medicine taste like lime and strawberry cordial. This wasn't a smart move on Mary's part.

Children should not be enticed into

taking medicine by referring to it as "candy," nor should they be allowed to take medicine on their own. In addition, you'll reduce the risk of your kids experimenting with medicine if you avoid taking it in front of them (remember, your kids imitate you). And be wary about giving a child medicine in the dark—it's too easy to grab the wrong bottle.

Also, be careful about carrying medicine in your purse. During the course of a hectic day, it may often be within reach of a young child. Warn Grandma about this, too. She may be more likely to be carrying prescription drugs and can probably use this reminder when the kids are around.

Instruct your pharmacist to use only child-resistant caps on your prescriptions. Check the label every time you give medication to your child. Put the child-resistant lid back on the container; don't leave open on sink or counter. Be sure to complete the prescription, then throw away the container. Use child-resistant latches on storage cabinets in which medicine (prescription or over-the-counter) is kept.

Common household cleaners: common poisoning sources

Many poison ingestions can be prevented by keeping child-resistant lids on containers and keeping containers locked up. Use safety latches on drawers and don't use the cabinet under the sink to store cleaning supplies.

When buying toxic products, choose those with child-resistant caps (but remember, your child will watch you and eventually learn to open these). Read labels so you buy the least-toxic brands you can find. Don't store cleaning products in containers that were once used for food—it can be easy to confuse the two. Be aware that some food products can also be dangerous to children. Vanilla extract, for example, contains alcohol.

If your child should ingest a poison, be it medicine, cleaning product, or plant, call your local poison control center immediately. This number can be found on the inside cover of your phone book and should be posted on or near every telephone in your home. Always have on hand a small bottle of syrup of ipecac (used to induce vomiting). Use this product under the supervision of the doctor or trained professional who is on the other end of the line at the poison control center. Don't rely on the first-aid instructions printed on product labels. They may be inaccurate or out of date. You will get specific instructions for your child from poison control.

Nature's harsher side

Plants that lead the list of poisoning to children include philodendron and dieffenbachia (dumb cane), but more than 100 fairly common house and garden plants can cause stomach discomfort. Your regional poison control center can tell you how to obtain a list of these. ***If you don't know what a certain plant is, assume it is poisonous and keep it out of the house and garden.***

Teach children to enjoy and appreciate plants, but not to eat leaves, bulbs, seeds or berries, or play with them. Even nonpoisonous plants may be hazards when a baby knocks over a heavy flowerpot or eats soil that has been treated with pesticides.

Invisible dangers

Environmental toxins, especially lead from paint or water pipes and carbon monoxide, are a real threat to families today. Small doses of lead exposure can slow physical and mental development. Higher doses can be much more serious. Most lead ingestion results from ingestion of leaded dust and dirt and leaded paint chips. Leaded paint was banned in 1977, but remains on walls and woodwork in millions of homes. Water, carried by pipes made or soldered with lead, is another source of lead. It can also leach from old or imported pottery used for food. ***If you have a young child, or are pregnant, you should have your water at sink and kitchen faucets tested. Also ask your child's physician whether your child needs to be tested for lead. Guidelines are available from the EPA Lead Information Hotline, (800)424-LEAD. Your state health department can also give you information on lead poisoning.*** Have your water tested by an independent laboratory. The EPA's Safe Drinking Water Hotline (800) 426-4791 can direct you to a laboratory near you.

Carbon monoxide displaces the oxygen in the blood, causing lightheadedness, nausea, sleepiness, neurological problems, and even unconsciousness and death. It is an odorless, colorless gas that you can inhale without knowing that you've done so. Some cities have recently enacted carbon-monoxide detector laws that require landlords and homeowners to install detectors, much like smoke detectors, that beep shrilly and warn occupants should gas be seeping from a heating unit or other source. Your carbon monoxide detectors should be UL-approved. Place in every sleeping area, on the ceiling at least 15 feet from fuel-burning appliances. Also, space heaters, furnaces, fireplaces, and wood-burning stoves should be vented properly and inspected by a professional annually. Replace air filters in forced-air heating systems, and never use a barbecue or hibachi indoors.

TAKING ACTION to prevent poisoning:

- Keep medicines in child-resistant containers and in a secured cabinet.
- If your child should ingest a potential poison, be it medicine, cleaning product, or plant, call your local poison control center immediately.
- Don't store cleaning products or any potentially poisonous substances (such as lighter fluid) in an empty beverage bottle or can — not even for "just a second."
- Test your water for lead, and your child for lead poisoning.

Preventing Choking

Choking is the fourth leading cause of accidental death among young children in the home and, according to the American Academy of Pediatrics (AAP), the most common cause of accidental death in children under age 1. By avoiding foods that cause choking, keeping common household objects from a child's reach, and knowing what to do should a child start to choke, you can guard against a choking accident.

A Top Nine list

The American Red Cross says that the most common culprits for choking in children under 4 years include:

- Popcorn
- Grapes
- Nuts (especially peanuts)
- Hard candies
- Raw vegetables (like carrots, sliced into circles)
- Deflated balloon pieces
- Small items (like coins, pins, buttons)
- Small toys and removable or loose toy parts
- Small circular pieces of hot dogs

This list can be puzzling for parents who see their 2- or 3-year-old handling food and feeding more and more efficiently, but ***until children reach the age of about 4 or 5 they haven't mastered the art of chewing and grinding that is necessary to eat small, hard, smooth foods*** such as peanuts (AAP recommends that children under 7 not be given peanuts) or grapes.

Other food and object hazards include raw celery, raw cherries with pits, spoonfuls of peanut butter, raisins, crayon pieces, marbles, jewelry, small batteries, eggshells, pop tops from beverages, and a broken or misused pacifier. Baby powder is not a choking hazard but an inhalation hazard to infants. You'll need to enlist the help of the entire family to keep such foods and objects out of your younger child's reach. Remind older brothers and sisters about these hazards. Small toy parts, especially accessories from action and fashion dolls, are hazards. Symptoms of

Food in a certain size and shape, such as carrots and hot dogs, can easily become lodged in the throat. Items such as these can be quartered before slicing horizontally. This reduces the risk a great deal, but NOT entirely.

foreign objects stuck in the throat or esophagus are gasping, gagging, and turning blue.

In the event your child does choke

If your child starts to choke, don't panic. If he is distressed, but can cough, speak, or breathe, don't interfere. This is the natural way to remove an object that's obstructing airways.

But if your child makes the international distress sign for choking, putting both hands to the throat, or if your infant turns from bright red to blue, you must ask someone to call 911 while you administer CPR. Children over age 1 receive the Heimlich maneuver (or a modified Heimlich if the child is small). Infants receive blows to the back in a procedure with specific guidelines. Talk to your doctor or contact your local chapter of the American Red Cross for specific instruction on how to help a choking child. Remember, too: have somebody call 911, fast!

Vigilance is key

Don't leave babies alone to eat or suck, or young children to eat or drink. You should be there to monitor their needs. Babies should always be held while being fed. Don't let your kids play games that involve pouring or throwing drinks or candy into their throats. Don't let them eat while running and playing. Don't force food into a child's mouth. Don't let children (of any age) suck hard candy or eat anything while lying down.

TAKING ACTION to prevent choking:

- Don't let your children under 5 eat small, hard, smooth foods such as popcorn or grapes.
- Learn the Heimlich maneuver so you can help a choking child. Know that there are different maneuvers for infants/young children.
- Don't leave babies alone to eat or suck, or young children to eat or drink.

Miscellaneous Hazards

One of the downsides of progress is that it creates new hazards for parents to guard against. Twenty-five years ago, automatic garage door openers and mini-blind cords weren't there to pose a hazard; today they are.

We've suggested that you take a good look at what's already in your home, but remember also to examine carefully anything new that becomes a part of your household furnishings or outdoor equipment. Children are experts at figuring out how to play with something that's not a toy—don't discourage their flights of fancy, but do make sure they're safe while exercising their imaginations.

Trouble in toyland

Toys and toy chests can pose hazards for your children. Use common sense in choosing your child's toys. The manufacturer's age guidelines are designed to educate parents to look out for the safety of their children.

Older toy chests pose two dangers: serious injury or death should the lid fall on a child's head or neck, and suffocation, should your child climb in and become trapped in an older, unventilated model.

Think about displaying toys on low shelves or piling them in a plastic laundry basket, instead of using a toy chest. ***But if you use a toy chest, be sure it has a hinged top that stays open in any position and can't be latched shut, and that it has space between the lid and the chest and/or ventilation holes to guard against suffocation.***

According to the Consumer Product Safety Commission (CPSC), more children choke to death on balloons than on any other toy. Keep uninflated balloons and pieces of broken balloons away from children. If your child is injured on any toy or if you find a toy that

seems unsafe, report it to the CPSC at (800) 638-2772. (You can also call the CPSC to check on current product warnings and recall notices.)

Other common toy hazards include: rattles that are too small—they should be at least 1 5/8 inches across; squeeze toys where the squeaker is easily detached; stuffed animals with eyes or nose attached loosely or ribbons wound round the neck; electric toys (children under 10 should not play with anything that must be plugged into an electric outlet—buy battery-operated toys instead); noisy toys—besides driving parents crazy, cap guns, squeeze toys and other toys with a noise level at about 100 decibels can damage hearing; and projectile toys, which can cause eye injury. Use headsets with a decibel control setting.

A salute to progress

In 1973, the federal government enacted safety standards for cribs, including regulations for manufacturers that ***crib slats must not be set more than 2 3/8 inches apart, and that crib mattresses must not be more than 5 inches thick and must fit snugly in the crib so that not more than two adult fingers fit between it and the sides of the crib.***

New cribs should automatically meet these standards, but problems may occur if you are using an older crib. You and your siblings may have had plenty of sweet dreams in it, but the old crib's slats may be too far apart. Take a tape measure and doublecheck that it's safe. If it's not, you should purchase a safe, new crib. If you must use a used crib, inspect and measure carefully to make sure it meets safety standards. Your child's crib should not have head or footboard cutouts. An infant's head could get caught in these. Also, crib corner posts (also called finials) should not extend more than 1/16 inch above the top of the end panel. They could become catchpoints for your child's clothing and cause strangulation.

Strangulation hazards (blinds, shades, drawstrings)

In the past 20 or so years, more than 350 children have strangled in the cords for blinds or other window coverings.

The Window Covering Safety Council and the CPSC urge parents to ***remove the loops in the cords of blinds and shades and add a special tassel that can be gotten at a window-covering dealer.*** Do this three-step process:

1. Cut the cord above the end tassel.
2. Remove the equalizer buckle.
3. Slip tassels onto the two new cords that you have created.*

*For free tassels, call the Window Covering Safety Council at (800) 506-4636.

CPSC has also issued warnings about the dangers of drawstrings from the hoods and necks of children's clothes. During the past 15 years, at least 21 children have died and 42 have been injured when their drawstrings got caught on cribs, escalators, fences, and playground equipment, especially slides. If any of your children's clothes have drawstrings around the hood or neck, remove them. Never allow your children to wear necklaces, purses, scarves or clothing with drawstrings while they are at the playground. Also, don't hang anything on or above a crib with a string or ribbon longer than seven inches.

Open sesame—garage door accidents

CPSC also urges parents to ***disconnect and replace operators on garage doors that do not reverse upon striking an object.*** Make sure the control switch on your automatic garage door is high out of reach of children and that the remote control is locked away.

To market, to market ...

For most parents, the grocery store often feels like home away from home—to this end, you need to be aware of the potential dangers of shopping carts. Carts have a narrow wheel base and are easy to tip over. Children may suffer cuts, bruises, fractures, concussions and internal injuries when they fall or jump from a shopping cart.

The National Safe Kids Campaign reports that the number of children ages 5 and under who are injured in shopping-cart-related incidents has increased 30 percent in the past 15 years. Your best defense against becoming part of this statistic is to never let your child stand in a shopping cart, always use the safety belts to restrain your child in the cart and don't let your child push or steer the shopping cart. Most important, always stay close to your cart when your child is in it. Watch her closely so that when you're reaching for a loaf of bread, she's not standing up and leaning out of the cart, trying to get to the cookies.

TAKING ACTION to prevent injury from miscellaneous hazards:

- Make sure your toy chest has a hinged top that stays open in any position and can't be latched shut, and that it has space between the lid and the chest and/or ventilation holes to guard against suffocation.
- Check that the slats on your child's crib are not more than 2 3/8 inches apart and that the mattress fits snugly to the crib sides and is not more than 5 inches thick.
- Remove the loops in the cords of blinds and shades.
- Disconnect and replace automatic garage doors that do not reverse upon striking an object.

SECTION II

Safe and Sound Outside the Home

Our children, any age, spend plenty of time outside the home, whether it's driving to school with Mom, shopping with Dad at the grocery store, climbing the play structure at the playground, or camping with the family.

When our kids are out of the house, they're automatically exposed to another set of potential hazards. The alternative to encouraging them to get outside and explore and create independent lives—keeping them in the house until they're mature enough to have kids of their own—isn't possible. Instead, we have to teach them how to live safely, provide supervision whenever necessary, and keep our fingers crossed.

In this section, we'll look at what we can do to protect our kids from car crashes, strangers, and typical vacation hazards.

Motor Vehicle Accident Prevention

Motor vehicle accidents are the leading killer of children under 14. The National Safe Kids Campaign reports that in 1996, for instance, 1,813 children died in motor vehicle crashes, and in 1997, 282,000 children were injured in accidents with automobiles. But by using child safety seats correctly, driving safely and defensively, and teaching your child how to be a smart and cautious pedestrian, you can greatly lessen the chance of injury by automobile.

No exception to this rule—using infant and child safety seats

From the first time we drive our newborn home from the hospital, he or she must be properly restrained when in the car. This is a rule without exception, and it's the law in every state.

Some people think there's no place like Mom's or Dad's arms when a baby is traveling in a car, but even a minor collision can result in an infant being torn from a parent's arms or being crushed against the dashboard by that same parent's weight. The extra minute we take to strap our infant, toddler or older child in safely may save his or her life should there be even a minor fender bender.

But child safety seats and other restraints that are used incorrectly do no good at all. According to the National Highway Traffic Safety Administration (NHTSA), as many as half of the child safety seats in use today are installed

incorrectly, without parents realizing it. Infants (birth to 20 pounds) should ride in a semi-reclined, rear-facing child safety seat in the back seat. And airbags can injure and kill older children, too. Always buckle the child safety seat harness and make sure it fits snugly against the child. Anchor the child safety seat with the vehicle safety belt. Follow the child safety seat manufacturer's instructions exactly for securing the seat and your child in it.

Infants and children 12 years old and under should sit in the back seat and always be properly restrained. Adults and older children who sit in the front seat should adjust their seat far back from the airbag.

Toddlers (20 to 40 pounds) should ride in a forward-facing child safety seat in the back seat. Again follow the manufacturer's instructions for buckling up your child and anchoring the seat in the car.

If you need to shorten lap belts that do not lock and secure your child safety seats, you will need a special belt-shortening clip. According to NHTSA, this heavy-duty locking clip is available only from Ford, Toyota, and Nissan dealers. Also, it must be the heavy-duty clip, at least 3 inches long and made from extra-strong metal. If you have questions about how to use locking clips or about keeping your child restraint systems tightly secured, call your vehicle customer service line.

Children may move on to booster seats used in conjunction with safety belts when they are about 40 pounds or 40 inches (often at about 4 years). Call NHTSA (800) 424-9393 for more information about safe child safety seats and other restraints for your children.

When your child outgrows the booster seat, insist upon consistent use of the three-point safety belt, even for short trips. The lap belt should fit snugly as low as possible across a child's hips, with the shoulder belt crossing across the child's shoulder and chest, not face or neck. If the shoulder belt does not fit properly, the child should remain in a booster seat until it does.

New system introduced

The Universal Child Safety Seat System (UCSSS) is a uniform anchorage system for all new cars and child safety seats. In the car, the UCSSS consists of two lower anchorages and one upper anchorage. Each lower anchorage will be a rigid, round rod or bar located where the seat cushion meets the seat back. The upper anchorage will be a ring-like object, permanently attached to the vehicle at the top of the rear seat. The child safety seat will then have a hook, buckle or other connector that snaps onto the lower anchorage bars in the car. A tether strap from the top of the child safety seat will be attached to the upper anchorage in the car.

Your old child safety seat is still safe and you should continue to use it if you do not buy a new car that has the UCSSS. The UCSSS is only trying to help fix the problem of incorrectly-installed child safety systems. Also, the new child seats can be used in your older car.

For cars and child safety seats manufactured on or after Sept. 1, 1999, the UCSSS will be phased in. By Sept 1, 2002, all new vehicles and child safety seats will be equipped with the UCSSS.

Your child learns by imitation. Always buckle up and insist that other adult passengers do, too. An unrestrained passenger becomes a flying missile during a crash, causing serious injury.

Driving through distractions

Your child is safest in an automobile driven by a careful, experienced driver, who acknowledges his or her responsibility behind the wheel, especially when driving children. Of course, with or without children in the car, no one should ever drive under the influence of alcohol or drugs. If you're involved in a carpool, make sure you are confident about the other drivers and their cars. Do they have appropriate restraints for every child in the car? Two to a safety belt is unsafe and unacceptable.

Insist on good behavior in the car, especially with a group of children. Clear the dashboard and back window ledge of all objects. In a crash, they may turn into projectiles, or kids may be tempted to throw them, should horseplay get out of hand. Pick up and let off kids only in their driveways or at

the curb. When they get in and out of the car, be sure to watch out so fingers are not smashed in the door. Limit noise and disruption—be firm with kids before the trip starts. You're a safer driver when you don't have to worry about events *inside* the car.

Preventing Pedestrian Injury[1]

Because children from ages 5 to 9 want to enjoy their independence before they are ready, they are particularly vulnerable to pedestrian accidents. Safety messages directed to children in this age group and to their parents should help children build on their sense of independence by giving them specific actions they can take to ensure their safety, yet help them feel in control of their own well-being.

Teach children ages 5 to 9 the following safety messages:

- Stop before entering the roadway—either at the curb, the edge of the road if there is no curb, or the outside edge of an object, such as a parked car, that might be blocking their vision.
- Stop before crossing a driveway. If a vehicle is turning into the driveway, teach children to let it pass before continuing across.
- Never play in a street or driveway.
- Recognize the people who can help them cross the street safely—safety patrol, adult crossing guard, parents, older brothers or sisters—and cross only with these people.
- Look left for approaching vehicles, look right, and then look left again to check for a gap in traffic. If a vehicle is coming or turning into a driveway, teach children to let it pass. Then look left, right, and left again before crossing.
- Check for approaching traffic—even after the school crossing guard has indicated it's okay to cross—by looking left for approaching vehicles, looking right, and then looking left again. Keep looking while crossing. The crossing guards may direct traffic or look for gaps in traffic large enough for children to cross safely.

[1]Courtesy: Walk Alert. A joint project of National Safety Council, National Highway Transportation Safety Administration and American Automobile Association.

- Look over their shoulders at intersections to check for turning vehicles.
- Recognize relevant traffic signs (such as advance pedestrian crossing and school crossing), signals, and crosswalks, and know what each means.
- Stay out of the way of vehicles, particularly emergency vehicles.
- Wear fluorescent or bright-colored clothing at all times, especially at dawn and dusk, to help drivers see them.
- Stand back from the roadway while waiting for a school bus until the bus has completely stopped.
- Check to see that no cars are coming from the right before stepping off the school bus.
- After getting off a school bus, take three giant steps away from the bus, staying on the sidewalk. If there is no sidewalk, stay on the shoulder of the road. Never walk next to the bus. Make sure the bus driver sees that they are safely away from the bus.
- Before crossing in front of a school bus, take five giant steps beyond the front bumper of the bus, so the bus driver can see them.
- Stop at the far edge of the school bus as they begin crossing. Teach children to look left for approaching vehicles, look right, and then look left again. Keep looking while crossing. Encourage them to make eye contact with the bus driver, or any other driver, to be sure the motorists see them.
- Never go near the bus when it is moving. If they drop an object near the bus, they must tell the driver and follow the driver's directions. Wait until the bus is gone and no traffic is coming before picking up the object. Never reach under the bus.
- Walk, do not run, across a street.
- Never cross the street diagonally. Doing so increases the risk of pedestrian accidents.

Teach adults the following safety messages:

- Never allow children ages 5 to 9 group to cross busy streets alone.
- Never allow children in this age group to cross any street alone at night.
- Designate safe play areas for children away from the street and driveways.
- Demonstrate crossing the street correctly by first stopping at the curb and looking left for approaching vehicles, then right, and then left again. Keep looking while crossing. At corners or near driveways, always search for turning cars crossing their path.

Walkable America

Currently, the National Safety Council and NHTSA have joined forces to create and promote the Partnership for a Walkable America. In an effort to increase pedestrian safety, they suggest that parents take a walk with their children and rate how "walkable" their community is. You can receive a copy of the walkability checklist by contacting either organization (see Resources at end of book) or by visiting the NSC Web site at www.nsc.org.

TAKING ACTION to prevent motor-vehicle-related accidents:

- Place your children in the back seat of the car in a restraint system that matches their weight and height and that is used exactly in accordance with manufacturer's instructions.
- Insist on good behavior in the car, especially when driving a group of kids.
- Teach your children to stop, look left, right, left, and listen every time they cross any street.

Child Abduction Prevention

It is every parent's worst nightmare—their child is abducted. It is a scenario so painful you want to ignore it, not even think about it, not even read the next sentence here. But thousands of children are abducted by non-family members each year, and your best defense, your child's best defense, is acknowledging the danger and practicing safe routines to guard against this most frightening possibility.

Some general notes about child abduction: girls are more likely to be abducted than boys, but boys can be victims, as well. The primary reason children are abducted is for sexual molestation, followed by intent to murder. The National Center for Missing and Exploited Children (NCMEC) reports that most abductors are white males between the ages of 20 and 40; abductors may use force to overcome children, but they may also try to be friendly and elicit a child's trust.

Your child's best defense is knowledge

Children of any age can be taught to protect themselves against abduction. The format of the lesson depends on the age and maturity of the child, but from a very young age a child can be taught to say "no" to strangers and ***not to talk to***

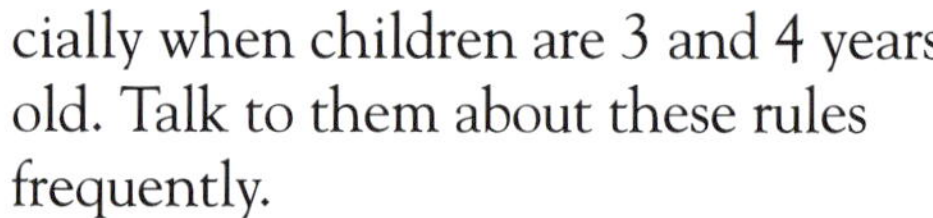

strangers. Or, as child development expert Penelope Leach suggests, teach your child not to go with strangers, and, especially, ***never to get in or near a stranger's car.*** As Leach notes, this is a more realistic lesson, since your child sees you talking to strangers every day and will learn valuable socialization skills by being friendly to people she's never met before.

Teach your child that you must always know where she is and that she must ask your permission first before she goes anywhere. This lesson can begin at a very young age when you take your child to the park. If she's playing in the sandbox and wants to go over to the slide, she must come to you on the park bench and ask permission to do so.

Repetition is key, especially when children are 3 and 4 years old. Talk to them about these rules frequently.

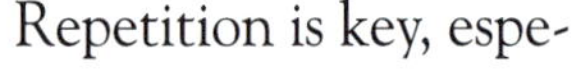

Practice role-playing exercises with your 5- or 6-year-old to address such situations as getting separated from you in a crowd or a busy store. Teach your child to stay in the place where you were last together, and ***not to go away with*** an adult who may come forward and offer to help her find Mom or Dad. Teach her that a kind and responsible adult will understand when she says "no" and will instead stay with her until you return or will summon help.

Let your child know which strangers she can talk to if she needs help—the uniformed police officer, the uniformed store security guard, the uniformed clerk who wears a name tag, and if necessary and no "official" help is around, a parent of other small children. Encourage your children to say "NO" loudly if ***anyone,*** uniformed or not, approaches them and makes them feel uncomfortable.

Children are kind—they'll want to help an unknown adult who asks for directions or claims they must come along because their parents need them. Remind them that trustworthy adults don't ask children for help. They should move away from such adults. Teach them to fight, kick, scream, and squirm if somebody tries to grab them. In such an instance, one child safety expert suggests you tell your children to shout "this is not my parent" to alert bystanders that an abduction, and not a tantrum, is taking place.

Don't let your child wear clothing that states her name, and teach her never to tell a stranger her name when she is alone. Beware of adults who show inappropriate interest in your child—wanting to play with her alone or giving her gifts. Encourage and remind your child to tell you about ***anything or anyone*** that makes her worried or uncomfortable. Such communication is your best defense should someone be watching your child in preparation to abduct her. Always carry a recent photo of your child, should she become lost or abducted.

As your child gets older, you can begin to pose "what if" situations to her and ask her what her response and action would be. Work with her to come up with the best response to a situation. Your child's best defense is her good judgment, something you can inform and encourage by talking to her.

Parents also need to be aware of danger on the Internet. The NCMEC launched a CyberTipline in March 1999 to field reports regarding child pornography, online enticement of children, and other incidents of child sexual exploitation. Don't allow your child's photo or first and last name to be published on the Web, either from a personal home page or a school Web site. We'll address other Internet safety issues later in this book.

Parents have a justifiable fear that all this talk and instruction will make their children fearful. But authorities nationwide agree that parents have no choice but to warn their kids of the real dangers that exist. When you talk to and teach your children about abduction, remind them that it's not a common occurrence, but that by learning about this danger, they'll become safer, stronger, and more confident.

If your child goes to a day-care center, be sure to give center staff clear instructions if you give anyone else permission to pick up your child.

When the danger is Dad or Mom

According to the Department of Justice, about 350,000 abductions per year are committed by family members. Most of these kidnappers are divorced parents who lost a custody fight. Protecting your child from this kind of abduction is even more difficult than teaching them about the dangers of strangers.

If you suspect your ex-spouse may try to kidnap your child, you should

talk to school officials and teachers and remind them that she can only be released to you or a person you designate. During this time, don't send your child to school on the bus or on foot. Arrange to drive her and pick her up yourself or delegate this task to a trusted family member or friend.

Talk to your child about the divorce. If you have real concerns about abduction, explain how much you love her and that the court has decided she should live with you, and then inform her about what her noncustodial parent might do. Remind her that you love her unconditionally and that you always want her to be with you. Her noncustodial parent may try to tell her that you no longer want her to live with you; tell her not to believe this; that even if her other parent or anyone else says so, this will never be true.

TAKING ACTION to prevent abductions:

- Teach your child never to go with strangers, and especially never to get in or near a stranger's car.
- If you are going through an acrimonious divorce, talk to school officials and teachers and remind them that your child can only be released to you or to a person you designate.

Vacation Safety

Vacations are funny. They're supposed to be great escapes—a time to relax, to enjoy, to have fun, to explore—but for the unprepared or careless family, they can be an invitation for accidents to happen.

Whatever jurisdiction your family is in—beach resort, campground, foreign country—the safety rules apply when on vacation. Your hotel room or tent is your temporary home. Examine it for potential hazards to your children.

Prepare your kids before you leave home by reminding them of the basic rules regarding strangers, water safety, and child safety seat use. In addition, the city kid will need some guidelines before he goes camping so he doesn't innocently pick up every snake he sees or wander off the trail. Likewise, the rural kid on his first trip to the city needs a lesson about safety on public transportation and a hint of the crowds and traffic he's going to encounter. Talk to your kids about the new situations they're likely to face.

Hot fun in the summer sun

All of the basic water safety rules you've taught your child—don't swim alone, wade in first, don't run on the pool deck, don't jump on others—go double while on vacation and swimming in unfamiliar territory. A child who has never swum in the ocean needs a lesson on the strength of the waves and the undertow, and, of course, all children swimming anywhere need constant vigilance by an adult.

In your zeal to chart new territory, you may find an unpatrolled, deserted part of the beach. Be wary about swimming there. ***A beach or pool monitored by you and a lifeguard is safest for your child.*** See Section III for more on water safety and how to guard against drowning.

You also need to be vigilant about using sunscreen. If you protect your child's skin, you can decrease his risk of skin cancer by close to 80 percent. For children 6 months or older, apply a sunscreen with a sun protection factor (SPF) of 15 or above about half an hour before they go outdoors. (A new 1999 policy from the American Academy of Pediatrics (AAP) says it may be safe to use such sunscreen on infants younger than 6 months, applying a small amount on the baby's face and the back of the hands.) Be sure to choose sunscreen with extra staying power—ones that are waterproof, sweat-proof, or all-day—for your active children. Read the labels carefully and reapply as instructed.

When you're back from the beach, relaxing at the hotel, stay vigilant around the spa and hot tub. These are dangerous for young children, who can easily become overheated or drown in them. Don't allow your young children to use them.

Respecting Mother Nature on your family camping trip

Prior preparation is your best bet for

a safe, enjoyable camping and hiking trip. Be sure to pack clothes that can be used for dressing in layers, flashlights, matches, a first-aid kit, extra food supplies, maps, a watertight tent, warm sleeping bags, rain gear, and whistles that your children are instructed to use only if they are in danger or get separated from you.

Camp only in authorized campgrounds and always stay on the trail when hiking. Make sure the park ranger or appropriate authorities know your plans. Your children may move a lot more quickly than you do (remember, you'll have a much heavier pack on your back), and need to be reminded about the importance of keeping together on the trail. Remind them that if they do get separated, they should stay put and signal the group with the whistle. If you have a campfire, be sure to follow fire safety rules. Remember that sparks can fly.

Of course, as an adult, you should be well-versed in wilderness safety before you strike out on an ambitious camping trip. This includes being able to find shelter should unexpected weather hit, practicing stringent campfire safety, and having a basic knowledge of dangerous plants. Be sure to tell your children to avoid any animals they don't know—whether dogs, cats or wild animals.

When in Rome ... visiting foreign countries

Nothing can be more satisfying, or challenging, than travelling in a foreign country with your children. Their natural curiosity and sense of adventure may lead you to see things in a way you never would have on your own.

But it is much harder to guard against potential dangers in a foreign country—you're probably not familiar with the customs or the language. Your child won't be able to read signposts, directions, or street names should she become separated from you. And she won't understand what adults who may be trying to help her are saying. ***You must be extra vigilant to guard against your child getting lost.***

If you're visiting Great Britain or other countries where traffic flow is reversed, you and your children need repeated reminders to look the other way when crossing the street. This may be particularly confusing for your younger children, so keep a firm grip on their hands whenever you're crossing the street.

Of course, before you've left home, you must be sure that everybody has any necessary shots and vaccinations. And in some countries that are popular destinations, you won't want to drink the water or eat certain fruits or vegetables. Explain these rules to your children before you leave home and remind them frequently while travelling.

TAKING ACTION to insure vacation safety:

- Your hotel room or tent is your home away from home. Examine it for potential hazards to your children.
- Don't let your children swim alone.
- Camp and hike only in authorized campgrounds and always stay on the trail.
- When in a foreign country, be extra vigilant to guard against your child getting lost.

SECTION III
At Home or Away

Our kids face certain hazards that have a double edge, occurring in one form at home and another outside the home. For instance, a child can drown in a bucket of water that was just used to wash the kitchen floor, or she can fall into a friend's pool that doesn't have a secure gate around it.

In this section, we'll look at hazards including drowning, gun safety, and safe play.

Preventing Drowning

The National Safe Kids Campaign reports that drowning is the second leading cause of accidental injury-related deaths to children under 14. It happens in bathtubs and pools, buckets and toilets. It happens in seconds that will be remembered in slow motion forever. It can be prevented by following simple safety rules and procedures and by remembering that kids always need adult supervision when they are in or near water, at home or at the pool or lakefront.

But I just left for a second ...

Babies can drown in an inch of water and a few moments. When a small child finds his face submerged in water, instead of holding his breath, he'll breathe in deeply trying to get air, but instead pulling water directly into his lungs. Because babies' heads are so much heavier in relation to the rest of their bodies, they can't lift themselves up out of a bucket or toilet.

Do not leave standing water around the house. Empty buckets immediately—a baby can drown in an inch of water left behind after cleaning. Make a habit of always closing the toilet lid and the bathroom door. If your bathroom door locks from the inside, consider removing the lock to prevent accidental lock-ins, or drape a towel over the top of the door so your toddler won't lock himself in.

Many drownings and near-drownings occur when a child is

momentarily left alone in the bathtub. Never leave a baby or toddler alone in a bathtub, even for a second. Even a 2- or 3-year-old should not be left alone to bathe. If he slips under water, he needs to be pulled up fast.

A child in a bathtub takes priority over a ringing telephone or doorbell. If you must answer the phone, wrap the child in a towel and take him with you. And your older kids must be reminded to drain the water out of the bathtub immediately after bathing. A common scenario finds a toddler staring into the toy-filled, dirty depths of bathwater that older sis has just stepped out of—and toppling in face first.

Safety first, then fun—swimming and boating rules

Some parents think that a child is safe in a pool if she is securely placed in a flotation device, but this is not the case. These devices can give parents and kids a false sense of security. But the rule for pools is the same as that for baths— ***a child in water needs adult supervision at all times.*** No child should ever be left alone near a pool, and no child (or adult for that matter) should ever swim alone.

If your supervised child is using a flotation device, check that it follows standards set by the U.S. Coast Guard. Conservative water safety experts suggest that a child begin taking swimming lessons at about age 3. Though younger children can learn to swim, most parents report that they forget their swimming skills soon after the class ends. In the beginning, choose a

swim class that emphasizes water safety and safe play.

Parents need to be on guard against the overconfidence that can build up as their children progress through swim classes. No child has the consistent judgment and stamina to handle potentially dangerous situations—your 8-year-old may be winning ribbons in the local swim meet, but she needs to be watched whenever she's in water.

If you have a pool, install a minimum 5-foot-high fence on all four sides around the pool. Don't consider the house a side, especially if it has windows or doors that open to the pool area. The fence should have a self-latching gate that opens away from the pool. Children can drown in the water that accumulates on a saggy pool cover. Make sure the cover is secure all the way around the pool so the child cannot slip through and become trapped under the cover. Keep a life preserver or flotation jacket available and a rescue pole or rescue tube close to the pool. Install a poolside telephone and learn CPR so that you can respond to an emergency that may occur despite your best efforts. Prohibit running and rough play around the pool, and don't allow kids to dive in the shallow end.

Kids in boats should wear life jackets at all times. They should also be instructed about basic emergency procedures should there be an accident. These include staying with the boat or hanging on to something that floats, as opposed to trying to swim to far-off safety.

TAKING ACTION to prevent drowning:

- Don't leave standing water around the house.
- A child in water, be it a bathtub, pool, lake, or ocean, needs to be watched at all times.

Teach your children these four key rules of safe swimming: never swim alone; don't dive or jump into shallow or unfamiliar water, always wade in first; don't push or jump on others; be prepared for an emergency.

Internet Safety

Remember when your kid's superior technological skills centered on programming the VCR? Oh brave new world, that has such wonders as the Internet. Whether or not you enjoy being online, if you have children and a computer with Internet access, you need to become familiar with the World Wide Web. The Internet is a great place for you and your kids to find out more about almost anything—sports, history, nature, literature—but dangers lurk there and you and your kids need to be aware of them.

Many organizations are concerned with Internet safety. A coalition called GetNetWise (www.getnetwise.org) unveiled its Web site in July 1999 and offers many safety tips, including the ones below, to parents:

- Use the Internet with your kids. This way you can teach them how to be safe and responsible online.
- Teach them, remind them and emphasize, that they must never give out personal information (last name,

address, phone, where they go to school) to people they meet online, whether in a chat room, via e-mail, or on a family Web site.

- Place your family computer in a high-traffic space—the family room, or a large hallway.
- Don't allow your children unlimited time on the Internet and establish clear ground rules with them on sites they are not allowed to visit. Blocking and filtering programs are available and you may decide that one of these is appropriate for your family. But don't rely only on a filter. You need to know where your kids go on the Web.
- Remind your kids not to respond to offensive e-mail or chat room comments. Tell them not to open e-mail or downloaded files from people they don't know. Encourage them to get you immediately if they accidentally come upon a Web site, e-mail, or chat room that makes them uncomfortable. Assure them that you won't be angry with them, but that you need to know about anything that happens online that makes them uncomfortable.
- Remind them that people aren't always who they say they are on the Internet. Tell them never to arrange a face-to-face meeting with someone they've met on the Internet, and to tell you if somebody tries to arrange a meeting with them.
- Don't hesitate to contact the authorities if you are worried that your child or another child is in danger.

These simple steps can help insure that your kids surf the net safely. But remember, nothing substitutes for common sense and parental involvement. Your children's safe, healthy, full childhood depends upon many things — fresh air, play, reading books and spending time with friends and family— that they won't find at any Web site.

Guns and Safety

Many people feel "gun safety" is an oxymoron, but whether you're a handgun control supporter or a card-carrying member of the NRA, you no doubt agree that kids and guns don't mix. Period. Yet according to the National Safe Kids Campaign, 40 percent of all U.S. homes have some type of firearm and one in four have a handgun.

Some gun owners have unrealistic expectations and perceptions of how responsible children can and will be around guns. According to the Center to Prevent Handgun Violence (CPHV), a gun kept in the home for self-protection is 43 times more likely to be used to kill a family member, friend, or acquaintance than an intruder, and more than 1.2 million elementary-aged latchkey kids have access to guns in their homes. Though the American Academy of Pediatrics (AAP) and the CPHV *urge parents not to keep a gun in the house*, they suggest stringent safety rules if you feel you absolutely must.

If you own a gun

All guns, including BB guns, kept in homes with children should be stored unloaded in a locked container or other secure place, and should have a trigger lock. Bullets should be stored in a separate locked location. Many states have Child Access Prevention laws, which can hold adults criminally liable if they don't store guns and ammunition properly or use a safety device to lock their guns.

But whether or not your state has a law, always follow these rules:

- Always keep your gun unloaded.
- Place a trigger lock on your gun.
- Store your gun in a locked, secure place out of the easy access of children.
- Store bullets in a separate, locked location.
- Ask your police department for advice on safe storage and gun locks.

Even if you don't own a gun

As a parent, you have the responsibility to know if guns are present in homes where your child plays. You may be uncomfortable asking, and other parents may be unwilling to answer, but you must use the direct approach and ask other parents if they keep a gun in the home.

If the answer is yes, you may decide not to allow your child to play in that home as there is anecdotal evidence that a child is not safe in a home with a gun. Don't be embarrassed if you feel this way; simply state directly

TAKING ACTION to prevent injury from guns:

- Keep your gun stored, unloaded, in a locked container or other secured place out of reach of children, and be sure it has a trigger lock.
- Teach your children never to touch a gun, but if they see one, to leave the room immediately and to tell an adult.

that from now on, your child's friend will have to play at your house. Or you may decide that you will allow your child in the other home, providing the parents follow strict rules on gun safety. If this is the case, ask the other parents if they follow the gun safety storage rules listed above. If they refuse to follow the rules, don't let your child play in that house. Warn your children about guns in the home. ***Teach them that if they see a gun, they must not touch it, but must leave the room immediately and tell an adult.***

Sporting and Recreation Safety

A big part of providing children with healthy, happy childhoods is allowing them plenty of opportunity for outside play in the backyard, on playgrounds, riding their bikes, and in organized sports programs. But obviously, there are hazards involved anytime kids are running and jumping and having fun. They're more likely at these times to forget or ignore some of the basic safety rules we've taught them. But even outside, in a less-controlled environment, there are things we can do to lessen the chance of injury to our kids.

In the backyard

A child as young as 3 may be left alone to play in the backyard if it is entirely fenced in, the neighborhood is safe, you can see him from your window, and you check on him every few minutes. ***Before you let him play outside, do a thorough safety check together. Make sure he understands the potential hazards and proper safety procedures.*** Make sure he understands and can't wander onto a driveway, the street, or another person's backyard. Check that you've safely stored garden tools, and that any potential toxins such as pesticides, fertilizer, and leftover paint are safely locked away.

If you allow your kids to play out front, with supervision, you may want to invest in some simple safety cones so you can delineate the area in which they're allowed to play. Along with proper instructions from you, the cones help remind them not to dart into the street after a runaway ball or other toy.

More likely, you'll often be outside with your children when they're playing, but resist the temptation to kill two birds with one stone by mowing the lawn as they play. Lawn mowers and kids don't mix. Children should be indoors while you mow. The mower could throw sticks or stones with enough force to hurt them. And children should never operate a power mower or ride with you on a ride-on mower.

Expanding the boundaries for play

Playground play can be some of the most instructive fun your kids have. Climbing and swinging and sliding encourage kids to push their physical abilities. You can lessen the obvious dangers involved by examining the playground and making sure it's safe and by teaching your kids some basic rules and manners.

Make sure the playground has a soft surface under swings, slides, and jungle gyms—loose sand, wood chips, and rubber matting are all acceptable. Check wooden structures for splinters—make sure the surface is smooth. Inspect the equipment periodically. Look for and repair sharp edges, broken links on a chain, or rusted bolts.

Common courtesy also helps keep kids safe on playgrounds. Teach your child to swing safely—one to a swing, sitting in the middle of the seat—and never to walk in front of or behind a swing while someone else is on it. They also need to learn to wait their turn for the slide.

And even though playgrounds today are much safer and more child-friendly than they were 20 years ago, you still should supervise your child when he's there. Don't allow your child under 4 to use climbing equipment that is taller than he is without close supervision; always check the slide surface to see if it's too hot for use; and make sure your kids under 5 play on equipment separate from older kids.

Trampoline injuries jump up

The Consumer Products Safety Commission (CPSC) estimates that in 1996 there were 83,000 hospital emergency room visits associated with trampolines. Most of these were for children under 14 years of age. Accordingly, the AAP now recommends that trampolines not be used at home, indoors or outdoors.

The weather outside is frightful ...

Kids don't want to stay inside just because it's cold out. And when the snow falls, children are more eager than ever to play outside. ***Be sure they're dressed properly— loose layers that allow air to circulate provide the best insulation.*** And pay particular attention to their extremities—a warm hat, good boots, and gloves or mittens are essential when children are outside in the cold. If your child complains of numbness of the fingers, hands, nose, toes, or feet, or if her skin is extremely red, bring her inside right away.

Go team

Playing organized sports, whether on a school, YMCA, or other neighborhood team, can be a big boost to your child's physical development and self-esteem and can help her learn social skills that will last all her life. But a child in a program where she's pressured to win, or a child who is forced to play a sport that doesn't interest her at all, may cause more harm than good.

Before you allow or encourage your child to join a team, learn something about the sport she wants to play. That way you can talk to her about it and prepare her for it. It also makes good sense to have your pediatrician give her a complete exam and to check her vision and hearing to rule out any potential problems that could be compounded by playing the sport.

Although the stereotype of the overinvolved Little League parent is brought to life on baseball diamonds across the country, you can be (and should be) informed and involved in your child's sports program without being everybody's nightmare. ***Talk to your kid's coach, about his or her approach. Are the kids grouped by weight, size, and skill level? (At early ages, they should be.) Are they encouraged to have fun, not pressured to win? (This is good policy at any age.)*** Make sure the coach is certified in CPR and has easy access to a telephone during practice and competition. A first-aid kit should also be on hand. Also, be sure the kids have

safety equipment that is approved by the National Operating Committee on Standards for Athletic Equipment (NOCSAE).

Protective equipment—helmet how-to's

One of the most important gifts you can give your skateboarding, rollerblading, or bike-riding child is the absolute rule: ***Never ride or glide without a helmet.*** Rollerbladers should wear a helmet, wrist guards, and elbow and knee pads. Injuries to wrist, elbows, and knees are becoming more and more associated with rollerblading.

Broken bones heal, but a head injury can lead to death or permanent disability, and head injury is the leading cause of death in bicycle crashes. The National Safe Kids Campaign reports that helmets reduce the risk of head injury by 85 percent and the risk of brain injury by almost 90 percent.

Only buy a helmet that has a seal of approval from the Snell Memorial Foundation, the American National Standards Institute (ANSI) and/or the American Society for Testing and Materials (ASTM). Make sure the helmet fits correctly and is easy for your child to use—kids might take off a helmet that's uncomfortable. Get your child invested in the process by letting him help choose the helmet. Follow these steps for fit:

1. Sizes range from small to extra large. Try the helmet on your child—it shouldn't pinch, but it should be snug.
2. Each size comes with additional pads to fine-tune the fit. Use these to make sure the helmet is snug.
3. Adjust the straps. The helmet should cover the top of the forehead. It shouldn't rock back and forth or side to side. The straps will help you get it level and snug.

Buy a hard-shell helmet for children older than 2, but kids younger than 2 need a foam helmet. The hard shell is too heavy for their neck muscles to support. Make sure a foam helmet has a fabric covering, as foam can stick to the road's surface, causing neck injuries. The fabric allows it to slide. Check your child's helmet regularly to make sure it fits and that it's not cracked or damaged in any way. Replace a helmet that has been used in a fall or collision.

Two-wheelin' it

Bicycles are associated with more childhood injuries than any other product except automobiles. As noted above, from the very start, your child needs to wear a helmet when cycling—no exceptions.

Most children are ready to handle a

tricycle at about age 3 and a two-wheel bike at about 7. Your child's tricycle should be built low to the ground with big wheels, giving it a stable base, which makes it harder to tip over. But remember: low-riding bikes are particularly hard for drivers to see. ***Don't allow your child to ride low-riding bikes near cars.***

Your children need to be reminded that fun as they are, bikes are not toys; even the law says they're vehicles, and as such, they have to follow rules just like cars and trucks. When your son rides in the street, he's a driver. Teach him these rules for safe biking:

- Stop and look in both directions for traffic every time you ride into the street from a sidewalk, parking lot, alley, or driveway.
- Ride as far to the right-hand side of the road as possible.
- Obey all traffic signs and lights.
- Always ride single file.
- Walk your bike across busy intersections.
- Before you turn left or right, look for traffic in front of and behind you.
- Use hand signals when you stop or make a turn: left arm straight out parallel to the ground for a left turn; left arm bent up at the elbow at a 90-degree angle for a right turn; left arm bent down at the elbow at a 90-degree angle for a stop.
- Only one person on a bike.
- Don't ride at dawn, dusk or night. The risk of injury during these times is nearly four times greater than during daylight.
- Keep your bike in good shape, especially the brakes.

TAKING ACTION to prevent sports and recreation injuries:

- Safety-check the backyard before you let your child out to play.
- Only allow your children to use playgrounds with a soft surface under swings, slides, and jungle gyms.
- Dress your children properly, in loose layers, for cold weather.
- Talk to your kid's coach and be sure that young children are grouped by weight, size, and skill level, and that all children are encouraged to have fun, not pressured to win.
- Never let your child ride or glide without a helmet and other protective gear.
- Don't allow your child to ride a low-riding bike near automobiles.

SECTION IV

If All Else Fails

Don't expect yourself to be perfect. You don't have eyes in the back of your head, unlimited reserves of energy, or the ability to match your child's ingenuity in inventing new ways to get in trouble. Accidents will happen. Serious accidents may happen. If they do, you'll have a better chance of dealing with them appropriately if you're prepared.

Calling 911

Talk to your kids about emergencies and 911. (Remember: some local areas do not use 911 for emergencies. Check your phone book or local police station to verify the emergency number for your area, and then post the number on or near every phone in the house.) A 4-year-old who is given plenty of repetitious instruction can perform admirably in an emergency. Explain to your children that 911 is not a toy or prank number. ***Discuss possible emergencies that may arise and when it would be appropriate to call 911.*** (For instance, the babysitter is unconscious or your child is accidentally locked alone in the house.)

Teach your child to state her name clearly and to tell the 911 operator that she is not playing with the phone. Remind her that the operator will need to know her address and phone number. While you're helping your child learn these, post them in large print around the house. Disconnect the telephone and practice with her—don't make it a game, make it a rehearsal. Reward her when she does a good job and do another run-through every few months.

First Aid and CPR

This book is about prevention. No parent expects or wants any of the accidents described in here to happen. But in the event that one does, a parent who knows basic first aid, the Heimlich maneuver and cardiopulmonary resuscitation (CPR) has a leg up on one who doesn't.

National Safety Council offices, chapters and training agencies, as well as Red Cross chapters, YMCAs, hospitals, and fire departments offer such classes at various times throughout the year. The Red Cross also offers "Basic

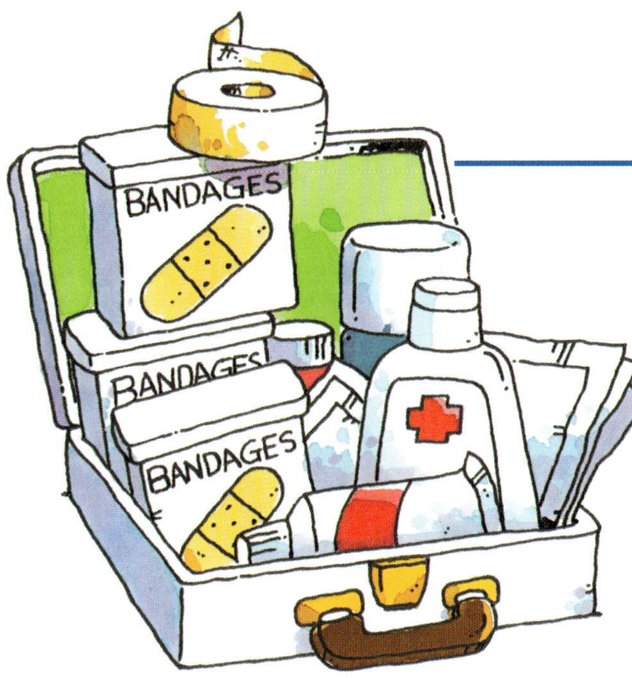

Aid Training" for children 9 years and older. Many of these courses are free or very reasonably priced—sign up for one as soon as you can. It could make a difference to you and your child for the rest of your life.

TAKING ACTION to be prepared for emergencies:

- Talk to your child about emergencies and when it would be appropriate to call 911.
- Post emergency phone numbers, including 911 and poison control, near every phone in the house.
- Learn basic first-aid procedures and CPR.

Conclusion

Our children, with their loving, curious, playful ways, are constant reminders of all that's good in life. And it's up to us to help protect them from all that's bad.

Teaching our kids basic safety procedures and urging them to take responsibility and use good judgment is the key to providing this protection without smothering them and making ourselves paranoid. Their safe childhood is a partnership between us and them. Supervise them directly—constantly when they are babies and toddlers, less so as they get older.

Keep the lines of communication open so you can help them develop the judgment and responsible attitude that will serve them best through their lives. This way, they'll take an active role in the process of keeping safe. With both of you working on it, your chances of success couldn't be better.

SUMMARY

Family Safety Checklist

This summary Family Safety Checklist highlights the basic advice offered throughout this book. Use it as a guide to keeping your kids safe. And add to it as necessary for your specific environment.

- Never leave your baby unattended, even for a second, when she is on an above-ground surface.
- Fit stairways with secure gates when your child begins to crawl and walk, and enforce the house rule: no game-playing on the stairs.
- Matches and lighters are tools, not toys—instruct your children to tell an adult if they find them lying around the house.
- Equip your home with smoke detectors, fire extinguishers, and a planned and practical fire escape plan.
- Keep medicines in a secured cabinet that your child can't reach.
- If your child should ingest a potential poison, be it medicine, cleaning product, or plant, call your local poison control center immediately.
- Don't let your children under 5 eat small, hard, smooth foods such as peanuts or grapes.
- Learn the Heimlich maneuver so you can help a choking child.
- Remove the loops in the cords of blinds and shades.
- Always place your children in the back seat of the car in an appropriate restraint system.
- Teach your children to stop, look left, right, left, and listen every time they cross any street.
- Teach your child never to go with strangers, and especially never to get in or near a stranger's car.
- When vacationing, examine your hotel room or tent carefully for potential hazards to your children.
- A child in water, be it a bathtub, pool, lake, or ocean, needs to be watched at all times.
- Don't allow your children to spend unlimited, unsupervised time on the Internet.
- Keep your gun stored, unloaded, in a locked container or other secured place out of reach of children, and be sure it has a trigger lock.
- Only allow your children to use playgrounds with a soft surface under swings, slides, and climbing equipment.
- Never let your child ride or glide without a helmet.
- Post emergency phone numbers, including 911 and poison control, near every phone in the house.
- Sign up for a course on basic first-aid procedures and CPR.

Bibliography

American Academy of Pediatrics. Press releases —"AAP Makes New Recommendations on Infant Use of Sunscreen," Aug. 2, 1999, and "Pediatricians Warn Against Dangers of Home Trampolines," May 3, 1999. Elk Grove Village, IL.

Center to Prevent Handgun Violence. Various fact sheets and safety steps posted on Web site: www.cphv.org. Washington, D.C.

Clausing, Jeri. "Industry Coalition Unveils Web Safety Effort," *New York Times*. July 30, 1999.

Consumer Product Safety Commission. Various publications including, "Your Home Fire Safety Checklist," "The Safe Nursery," and "Trampoline Safety Alert." Washington, D.C., 1999.

Environmental Protection Agency. *Protect Your Family From Lead in Your Home*. Washington, D.C., April 1999.

Fancher, Vivian Kramer. *Safe Kids: A Complete Child-Safety Handbook and Resource Guide for Parents*. New York: John Wiley & Sons, Inc., 1991.

GetNetWise. "Tips for Kids" and "Tips for Families." Posted on Web site: www.getnetwise.org.

Golant, Susan K. *Fifty Ways to Keep Your Child Safe*. Los Angeles: Lowell House, 1992.

Kane, Steven M., M.D. "Backyard Danger," *Parents*. August, 1994.

Karlsrud, Katherine, M.D., with Schultz, Dodi. "Bumps on the Head," *Parents*. January, 1994.

Laliberte, Richard. "Is Your Home Hazardous?" *Parents*. July, 1994.

Laskin, David. *Parents' Book of Child Safety*. New York: Ballantine Books, 1991.

Leach, Penelope. *The Child Care Encyclopedia*. New York: Alfred A. Knopf, 1984.

Mendels, Pamela. "Schools Careful About Posting Photos Online," *New York Times*. June 16, 1999.

National Center for Missing and Exploited Children. Various fact sheets and articles posted on Web site: www.ncmec.org. Alexandria, VA.

National Highway Traffic Safety Administration. *Child Transportation Safety Tips*. Washington, D.C. October 1998.

National Safe Kids Campaign. Fact sheets — various topics including bicycle injury (12/98), falls (12/98), unintentional firearm injury (12/98), drowning (12/98), motor vehicle occupant injury (12/98), shopping cart injury (12/98), burn injury (12/98), residential fire injury (12/98), poisoning (12/98), toy injury (12/98), airway obstruction injury (12/98). Washington, D.C.

National Safe Kids Campaign. *Safe Kids Are No Accident!* Washington, D.C., 1998.

National Safety Council. Fact sheets—various topics, including drowning (2/99), pedestrian safety (5/99) and poisoning (4/98). Itasca, IL.

Parents magazine. "Kids' Health and Safety" column. Monthly issues: Jan.-April, June-Sept., and Nov.-Dec. 1994; Jan. 1995.

Saunders, Carol Silverman. "The Gun Next Door," *Parents*. February, 1994.

Schneider, Phyllis. "Accidents You Can Prevent," *Parents*. January, 1995.

Schor, Edward L., M.D., Ed. The American Academy of Pediatrics *Caring for Your School-Age Child*. New York: Bantam Books, 1999.

Shelov, Steven P., M.D., Ed. The American Academy of Pediatrics *Caring for Your Baby and Young Child*. New York: Bantam Books, 1998.

Stepp, Laura Sessions. "Missing Children: The Ultimate Nightmare," *Parents*. April, 1994.

Resources for Additional Information

800 numbers and Web sites

(800) 638-2772 www.cpsc.gov	**Consumer Product Safety Commission (CPSC)** Information on a variety of consumer products such as smoke and carbon monoxide detectors, window covering pull cords and garage door openers. Recalls on such items as flammable clothing and toys.
(800) 424-LEAD Gen. Info.: www.epa.gov/lead Publications: www.epa.gov/lead/nlic	**EPA Lead Information Hotline** Information about lead poisoning and standards for testing children; information about contacts in your state and local health department.
(800) 424-9393 www.nhtsa.dot.gov	**National Highway Traffic Safety Administration (NHTSA)** Information on auto safety seats and systems, pedestrian safety, school bus safety, motor vehicles.
(800) 426-4791 www.epa.gov/safewater	**Safe Drinking Water Hotline** Environmental Protection Agency (EPA). Information on where to have water tested for lead.
(800) 505-CRIB www.nih.gov/nichd	**Sudden Infant Death Syndrome "Back to Sleep" Hotline** A service of the National Institutes of Health.
(800) 506-4636	**Window Covering Safety Council** Information on where to get free tassels to improve the safety of mini-blind pull cords.

Other Resources

(212) 642-4900
www.ansi.org

American National Standards Institute
Information on health and safety standards for many products.

American National Standards Institute
11 W. 42nd St. 13th Floor
New York, NY 10036

(630) 775-2075

National Safety Council
Information on CPR and first-aid training, various safety topics; catalog of materials.

www.nsc.org

National Safety Council
1121 Spring Lake Drive
Itasca, IL 60143

(202) 662-0600
www.safekids.org

National Safe Kids Campaign
1301 Pennsylvania Ave. N.W. Suite 1000
Washington, D.C. 20004-1707

______________ (fill in)

Your local poison prevention hotline.
(See the inside front cover of your phone directory.)

______________ (fill in)

Your local emergency medical treatment number.
(See the inside front cover of your phone directory.)

Index

911 17,44
Abduction 27, 28, 29, 30
Airbags. 23
Alcohol or drugs 24
American Academy of Pediatrics 4
Animals 32
Appliance cords. 8
Automatic garage-door openers 21
Baby walkers 5
Backyard 39
Balloons. 16, 18
Bathtub 35, 36, 46
BB guns 38
Bicycles 1, 42, 43
Blinds. 20
Blinds and shades 20, 21, 46
Boats 36
Brain injury 42
Burns 6, 9, 12
Campfire 8
Camping 1, 31, 32
Cap guns 19
Carbon-monoxide poisoning 12, 14, 15
Carbon-monoxide detector. 15
Child abduction 27
Child safety seats. 22, 23
Child-resistant caps, containers . 13, 15
Child-resistant latches 13
Children's clothing 20
Chimney 10
Choking. 2, 16, 17, 46
Cigarette lighters 8
Cleaners. 12
Cleaning products 46
Climbing equipment 40
Consumer Product
Safety Commission 18
Cooking 7
CPR. 17, 44, 45, 46
Crib. 2, 3, 19,46
Crossing the street. 25, 46
Curling irons 8
Drawstrings 20
Drowning. 31, 34, 35
Elbow and knee pads. 42
Electric transformers 9
Electrical wires. 9, 12
Electricity, electrical shock 8
Emergency phone numbers. 44, 46
Escape exits, plans 11
Eye injury. 19
Falls 2
Fertilizer. 39
Fire. 1, 2, 6, 9, 10, 12
Fire drill 6, 11
Fire escape plan. 10, 12, 46
Fire extinguisher 10, 46
Firearms 37
Fireplace. 9, 10
First-aid kit 32, 41, 45
Flotation device, jacket. 35, 36
Foam helmet 42
Garage door. 21
Gates 4, 5, 46
Grapes 16, 17, 46
Gun safety 34, 37, 38, 46
Hand signals 43
Hard-shell helmet 42

Head injuries 2, 42
Heating system 15
Heimlich maneuver 17, 44, 46
Helmet 42-43, 46
Hot dogs. 16
Hot liquid 7, 12
Hot tub 31
Hot water. 10
Household cleaners 13
Infant and child safety seats 22
Internet. 36-37
Ipecac 14
Irons 8
Jungle gym 40, 43
Lake 36, 46
Lawn Mowers 39
Lead 14
Lead Information Hotline. 14
Lead poisoning 15
Lifeguard 31
Light socket 8
Lighters 8, 12, 46
Marbles 16
Matches 8, 12, 46
Medicine 12, 13, 46
Microwave oven 7
Mini-blind cords 18, 20
Motor vehicle accidents 22
National Safety Council 44
Nuts 16
Ocean 31, 36, 46
Paint. 39
Paint chips 14
Peanuts 16, 46
Pedestrian 1,25
Pesticides 39
Plants. 12, 14, 15, 46
Playground. 39, 40, 43, 46
Poison 12, 13, 15, 46
Poison control center 14, 45, 46
Pool 35, 36, 46
Popcorn 16
Pottery 14
Power lines. 9
Prescription drugs 13
Pressure gates. 4
Projectile toys 19
Raisins 16
Rattles 19
Red Cross. 44
Rescue pole 36
Rollerblading. 42
Safety seats 22, 23, 24
Safety cones 39
Safety equipment. 42
School bus 26
Shades 20
Shoulder belt 23
SIDS. 6
Skateboarding 42
Slides 40, 43
Sliding glass doors 4
Smoke 11
Smoke detectors 6, 10, 12, 46
Space heater 9, 10
Sports. 39, 41
Sports and recreation injuries 43
Sports programs 39

Stairs 4, 5, 46
Steam burns 7
Stop, look, and listen 25-27
Stove burner 7
Strangers. 27-30, 46
Strangulation 19
Stuffed animals 19
Sudden Infant Death Syndrome 6
Suffocation 18, 21
Sunscreen 31
Swimming 31, 35, 36
Swimming and boating rules. 35
Swings 40, 43
Three-point safety belt 23
Toxins 12, 39
Toy chest 18, 21
Toys 16, 18, 46
Trampoline 40
Tricycle 43
Vacation. 30
Vacation safety. 30-33
Wall outlets 8
Water safety 30, 31, 34-36
Window covering 20
Window locks 4, 5
Woodburning stove. 9, 12